GLOUCESTER ILLUSTRATED
The City's Heritage in Prints and Drawings

Alan W. Ball

HALSGROVE

First published in 2001 by Halsgrove
Copyright © 2001, Alan W. Ball

ISBN 1 84114 119 4

British Library Cataloguing-in-Publication-Data
A CIP data for this book is available from the British Library

HALSGROVE
Halsgrove House
Lower Moor Way
Tiverton EX16 6SS
T: 01884 243242
F: 01884 243325
www.halsgrove.com

Printed and bound in Great Britain by
Hackman Printers Ltd, Rhondda.

CONTENTS

For Marion

A reworking of John Speed's map of Gloucester of 1610 by Thomas Dudley Fosbroke from his *Original History of the City of Gloucester* of 1819. Fosbroke added in the fortifications from Hall and Pinnell's map of 1780 (190x240).

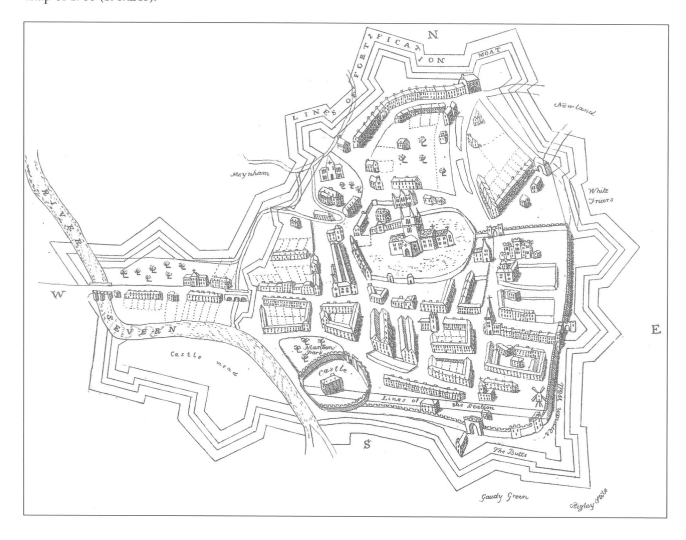

GENERAL INTRODUCTION

Gloucester was an important settlement in pre-historic times long before the arrival of the Romans because it was the lowest fordable crossing point on the Severn. The little tributary Leadon had brought down gravel to create a firm bottom in the river, which was divided at this point into two channels by the island of Alney, a natural feature that in large measure broke the force of the formidable tidal bore. It is ironic that the changes in contemporary communications have meant the railway tunnel and two road bridges on the M4 and M48, which link Bristol with South Wales, are well over 20 miles to the south and no longer depend on this original crossing point at Gloucester.

Although Cirencester appears to have been a more important Roman town than Gloucester, the latter controlled the route leading to the rich natural resources of the Forest of Dean in the territory of the extremely warlike Silures tribe. To subdue this threat the Roman station of Glevum was created and towards the end of the first century ad when this operation was largely completed, a colonia of time-expired legionaries was established either by Domitain or Nerva. Gloucester probably never achieved its full potential in Roman times, as it was overtaken not only by Cirencester, but later by Caerleon, which became the primary settlement for the defence of the South Wales frontier. However rather like York, Gloucester stands firmly on its Roman foundations and street pattern, as even after almost two thousand years a glance at the map of the City centre makes abundantly clear.

In Anglo-Saxon times a number of religious houses were founded in the City, but by the time of the Conquest many of these had declined to such an extent, that it could be said they barely existed. In 670 King Osric founded a house for both men and women in separate buildings on the same site, but four hundred years later this Abbey dedicated to St Peter had become a byword for luxury and lax living.

It is perhaps difficult at this long remove of time to realise what a whirlwind William the Conqueror let loose on England after 1066. High on his agenda was the reform of religious foundations and St Peter's Abbey was soon to feel the smack of firm government. Serlo, a chaplain to the Conqueror himself, was appointed Abbot of St Peter's in 1072 and set to work with a will. A new church was begun in 1089 and a sizeable part of the fabric had been completed by 1100. When Serlo died in 1104 he left behind a thriving community of a hundred or so monks and had turned round a decrepit foundation into an institution that was thriving and prosperous. This prosperity was greatly enhanced when the murdered King Edward II was buried there and it became an important place of pilgrimage. At the Dissolution the Abbey church was transformed into the present Cathedral, which was only saved from destruction at the time of the Commonwealth by the strenuous efforts of the then Town Clerk and local people.

After the Conquest Gloucester was favoured by many royal visits especially as William continued the previous practice of Saxon monarchs and summoned his nobles to keep Christmas in the City with much pomp and feasting. One less happy event for the whole populace of England was the holding of a witan by the Conqueror in Gloucester in 1085, at which the process of compiling the Domesday Book was set in motion in order to create an accurate basis for assessing taxation.

Not that it could be said that the citizens of Gloucester were overawed by royalty or those in authority. In the twelfth century anarchy of Stephen's reign the City supported the Empress and in the Civil War was on the Parliamentary side. For its part in the latter conflict, Charles II at the Restoration ordered the demolition of its defences.

The City played a prominent part in the creation of goods based on the excellent wool of Cotswold sheep and the manufacture of pins. As Gloucester expanded from the eighteenth century onwards, it ceased to be just a small cathedral city and developed an industrial base supported by wharf facilities on the shore of the Severn and later the dock area of the Gloucester and Sharpness Canal. While obviously not as important from the point of view of shipping as Bristol, nevertheless as late as the 1880s Mrs Schuyler Van Rensselaer in her book *English Cathedrals* was saying that of all the English cathedral cities she visited, none other than Gloucester had such a feeling of the nearby presence of the sea. 'Here we meet sailors in the streets, smell tar and fancy we smell salt; yet a pastoral and truly English country lies all around the town.' Today with the pre-eminence of road and rail communications the dock facilities naturally no longer have the importance of previous years.

During the course of the centuries a number of notable visitors came to the City and recorded their impressions. Among these were Leland the antiquary in the sixteenth century, Celia Fiennes and William Schellinks, a Dutch merchant, in the seventeenth century, Daniel Defoe and Arthur Young, the agriculturalist, in the eighteenth century and, with especially pungent comments William Cobbett in the nineteenth century. He arrived in Gloucester at the time of a Three Choirs Festival, which he referred to scathingly as a 'music meeting' and 'one of those assemblages of player-folks, half rogues and half fools'. He was outraged at what he had to pay for accommodation and he was even charged 9d by an ostler for allowing his horse to stand for ten minutes.

Obviously a number of artists visited the City, but it is not the object of this work to deal with original paintings or photographs, but the engravings, etchings and line drawings commissioned to illustrate books and periodicals. As these prints and engravings often appear at a different size from the originals, I have indicated the real dimensions in millimetres at the end of each caption with the height first and width second. Finally it should be made clear so much material exists, that careful selection has been the order of the day and I can only apologise in advance if many of your favourite illustrations do not appear.

Three seals of the City of Gloucester. The first and second show crude representations of the fortifications and the third features local manufactures. All are included in volume 13 of the *Transactions of the Bristol and Gloucestershire Archaeologial Society* of 1888/1889 (first 65x65 second 60x60 third 70x70).

DISTANT VIEWS

Winchester sits down in a hollow with the squat tower of the Cathedral making a distant view almost impossible, whereas Gloucester shares with Salisbury the wide vistas that come with an open landscape. The tower of Gloucester Cathedral is therefore a landmark across a vast sweep of countryside and in distant views it stands out clearly in the plain below the Cotswolds. The approach to the City from most directions gives a sense of anticipation as the principal buildings and especially the majestic Cathedral emerge into view, the nearer the visitor comes to the surrounding suburbs.

A view of Gloucester from Robins Wood Hill in what at the time was open country south of the City. It is dated 1791 and comes from Samuel Lysons' *Etchings of Views in the County of Gloucester Hitherto Imperfectly or Never Engraved* (82x130).

The ruins of St Oswald's Priory stand outside St Mary's Gate and were excavated in the 1980s. The Priory Church built in the first half of the twelfth century was demolished at the time of the Reformation, except for the north aisle, which was converted into a parish church dedicated to St Catherine, thus creating some confusion about the name. The artist of this view showing the Cathedral tower in the distance is Benjamin Baud and the engraver B. Winkles. It comes from volume three of H. and B. Winkles' *Cathedral Churches of England and Wales* of 1836 to 1842. The Winkles family had connections with a firm of steel engravers in Karlsruhe as early as 1832 and this new process allowed many more reproductions to be made than on the softer copper plates generally in use until the 1820s. The text of the work is by Thomas Moule, whose fame rests much more on his cartographic work (108x140).

An anonymous view from the west with the Cathedral dominating the City around it. It comes from Thomas John Bonney's *Cathedrals, Abbeys and Churches of England and Wales* of 1891. Bonney (1833-1923) was ordained in his youth, but is principally remembered as the Yates-Goldsmid professor of Geology at University College, London, from 1877 to 1901 (75x140).

An anonymous pastoral view of Gloucester from Castle Meadows to the South West of the City. It comes from the *Illustrated London News* of 16 July 1853 (145x230).

A north-west view of the cathedral by Herbert Railton from *Dreamland in History – the Story of the Norman Dukes* of 1891 by the then Dean of Gloucester, H.D.M. Spence (75x105).

A similar north-west view to that above by Joseph Pennell from Mrs Schuyler Van Rensselaer's *English Cathedrals* of 1887 (95x130).

Gloucester from the Severn, an anonymous view from the volume of the *Rivers of Britain* series entitled *Rivers of the South and West Coasts* published by Cassell and Company in 1897. The text of the section on the River Severn is by Thomas John Bonney (160x160).

A. Ward's version of Gloucester from the Severn in his undated *Sketches of Gloucester*, which appears to be of the early 1920s (100x100).

An undated drawing of Gloucester from the Severn by William Hyde, which is included in volume two of the *Victoria County History of Gloucestershire* of 1907 (140x205).

An almost identical view of that above. The artist is Joseph Pennell and it comes from Mrs Schuyler Van Rensselaer's *English Cathedrals* of 1887. The wood engraver is Charles State (105x132).

THE CITY CENTRE

The City centre of Gloucester follows the old Roman street pattern with four thoroughfares named after the cardinal points of the compass, each with the word 'gate' added. The defences including these gates were once almost as strong as those of Chester and York, but because Gloucester had sided with Parliament in the Civil War, Charles II ordered their destruction. The Westgate alone lingered into the second decade of the nineteenth century, but was removed to make way for Robert Smirke's new Westgate Bridge, while the medieval castle was replaced by a prison in the late eighteenth and early nineteenth centuries.

The Shire Hall, also by Robert Smirke dates from 1816 with alterations in the 1890s, extensions from 1909 to 1911 and further larger extensions in 1966. The Guildhall by George Hunt in a Renaissance style is of 1890 to 1892. There are of course the usual mostly Victorian public buildings such as the library, baths (extended in 1966), hospital and railway station. The Gloucester to Sharpness Ship canal, which was opened in 1827, created a dock basin with a Custom House, dock offices and warehouses and brought much more shipping into the City centre than the older riverside quay area.

Shops, pubs and hotels still have a surprising amount of older construction behind newer facades, but a great deal of what was built in earlier centuries has been swept away since the Second World War. However, the oldest and in many ways the saddest loss was the removal of the City cross from the intersection of the four main streets two and a half centuries ago, which merely goes to prove that urban 'improvers', like the poor, have always been with us.

Over Bridge still crosses the Maisemore Channel of the Severn in Gloucester immediately south of the dual carriageway of the A40 northern bypass, but now only leads to a path along the river. The bridge was built by Thomas Telford in 1825 and is based on a design by Perronet of 1768 for his bridge over the Seine at Neuilly. This undated view by J. Bellow of Gloucester is from a drawing by J. A. Smith and is included in volume one of *Gloucestershire Notes and Queries* of 1881 (115x180).

The High Cross which stood at the central crossroads in Gloucester and was removed as long ago as 1751 by civic 'improvers'. This engraving by George Vertue after a sketch by T. Ricketts is also of 1751. Vertue was one of the engravers to the Society of Antiquaries, in whose publication *Vetusta Monumenta* this illustration appears (450x300).

A reworking of Vertue's view lithographed for Charles Pooley's *Notes on the Ancient Crosses of Gloucestershire* of 1868 (140x90).

The so-called Old Judge's House at number 24 Westgate Street appears to be Georgian from the outside, but this is merely a later facade on what is a highly important timber framed building behind, which has important historical associations as it was occupied by Governor Massey during the siege of 1643. The sketch by E. J. Burrow of 1894 comes from H. J. L. J. Masse's *Cathedral Church of Gloucester* of 1898 (140x75).

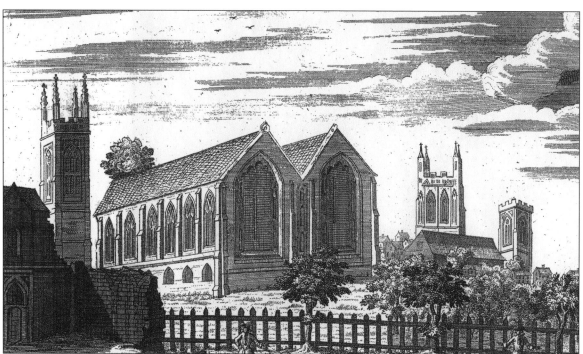

Another sketch by E. J. Burrow of 1894 showing the remains of a Roman wall under number 30 Westgate Street. It also comes from H. J. L. J. Masse's *Cathedral Church of Gloucester* of 1898 (75x60).

14

The remains of a toll house in Gloucester, which was partially destroyed by a violent lightning strike during a thunderstorm in June 1846. A number of people working in nearby fields ran into the building to take shelter and were knocked to the ground by the electrical discharge, although nobody was actually killed. This anonymous engraving of the partially destroyed toll house comes from the *Illustrated London News* of 4 July 1846 (100x150).

An anonymous engraving of a concert in the Gloucester Shire Hall showing the orchestra and soloists with the organ behind. It comes from the *Illustrated London News* of 24 September 1853 (150x240).

An engraving by Jewitt and Company founded by Orlando Jewitt, who died in 1869. It is of the Gloucester Co-operative and Industrial Society's then new stores on the corner of Brunswick Road and Barton Street, which were rebuilt in 1931. The engraving comes from the *Builder* of 24 November 1877 (170x275).

Messrs Fulljames and Waller's design for Schools of Science and Art in Brunswick Road completed in 1872. The Public Library was later added on the left side and the Price Memorial Hall (which became the Museum) on the right. This engraving by Worthington J. Smith comes from the *Builder* of 17 June 1871 (175x225).

A wonderful piece of fun by William Burges with his suggested fountain for Gloucester. In the background is Burges' imaginary view of the City in the thirteenth century, the lofty bell tower on the left being part of the town hall. The whole concept is based on the legend of the water sprite Sabrina and at the pinnacle an otter holds the City arms, frogs act as gargoyles while fish and lizards provide general decoration. The correspondent in the *Builder* of 29 May 1858, which carries this illustration writes 'Of course the background is unattainable at the present day, but there is no reason why the good citizens of Gloucester should not add a beautiful and useful adjunct to their famed Cathedral by executing the concept of Mr Burges in stone or marble' (270x180).

St Mary de Crypt School moved from Barton Street to Friars Orchard in 1889, where it was housed in a new building designed by Medland and Son. It moved yet again in 1943 when it was relocated on the Podsmead Estate. This view shows the original Barton Street building and comes from Albert Belden's *George Whitefield the Awakener* of 1953 (95x150).

The Old County Jail at Gloucester, which had been built on the site of the former castle.It had been demolished by the end of the eighteenth century and a new jail to replace it was constructed by William Blackburn in 1790 and completed after his death by the County Surveyor, John Wheeler. It was later enlarged in 1845 by F. Fulljames. This sketch of the original jail is by somebody simply called Mrs S– and it was redrawn and engraved by Thomas Bonnor for Thomas Dudley Fosbroke's *Original History of the City of Gloucester* of 1819 (85x135).

The original Abbey wall had the still existing gateway at the north west corner of the outer court. This is known as St Mary's Gate and leads into St Mary's Square. On the outside it has arcading over an arched entrance, both of the thirteenth century, and was restored by Waller and Son at the end of the nineteenth century. Above is a view drawn and engraved by Thomas Bonnor for Thomas Dudley Fosbroke's *Original History of the City of Gloucester* of 1819 (70x115). Below left is a sketch by F. S. Waller of 1852 for H. Haines' *Guide to the Cathedral Church of Gloucester* of 1867 (115x75). Below right is a drawing of the early 1920s by A. Ward for his *Sketches of Gloucester* (115x70).

Two sketches by F. S. Waller of 1852 from H. Haines' *Guide to the Cathedral Church of Gloucester* of 1867. Above is the one turret which survived from the gateway on the south side of the former Abbey precincts, the rest having been taken down when College Street was widened. It is known as King Edward's Gate. Below is a gateway with lierne vaulting leading from the outer to the inner court, the latter now called Miller's Green (both 115x75).

The gateway at the end of College Court was known as St Michael's Gate by the seventeenth century and is also called the Pilgrim's Gate. It appears to date from the end of the fifteenth century or possibly later and has a flattened arch flanked by two canopied niches. Above is a view by F. S. Waller of 1852 which comes from H. Haines' *Guide to the Cathedral Church of Gloucester* of 1867 (115x75), while that below is of the early 1920s by A. Ward from his *Sketches of Gloucester* (140x60).

Robert Smirke rebuilt Westgate Bridge from 1814 to 1816 with one span of 87 feet. It was initially a toll bridge, which caused great resentment and a tollhouse was demolished by a mob in 1827. Both these views are therefore nostalgic reminders of what the bridge looked like before that date and come from John Britton's *Picturesque Antiquities of the English Cities*. That above is after a painting by somebody simple called Pierce and the etcher is J. C. Varrall. It is dated 1 January 1830, but this is the date of the etching not the original art work. That below is after a drawing by John Carter of 1796 with no indication of a process worker and likewise the date of 1 July 1828 is more than thirty years after the sketching of the actual view. Both illustrations are full of life and vitality and repay a careful study of the large amount of detail. In 1447 the original bridge had four arches, by 1505 it was being described as 'a great bridge of freestone arched and embowed' and in 1643 parts of the structure were removed and replaced by a drawbridge. Floods and ice often caused damage and repairs became a regular item of Corporation expenditure (above 140x200 below 145x200).

Another view of Westgate Bridge before Robert Smirke's rebuilding of 1814 to 1816. This illustration is drawn and engraved by Thomas Bonnor for Thomas Dudley's Fosbroke's *Original History of the City of Gloucester* of 1819 (82x135).

The New Inn in Northgate Street of about 1457 belies its name and is one of the oldest surviving buildings in the City. It is said to have been built originally by a monk named Twyning to accommodate pilgrims visiting the shrine of Edward II in the Cathedral. Much of its original timber framing remains and it is constructed to a medieval plan with a courtyard and open galleries. In James I's reign it was important enough to have its own tennis court and displays its name in bold Victorian lettering. This view engraved by John Le Keux and dated 1 August 1830 is from an original drawing by William Henry Bartlett. It shows a chambermaid in the gallery looking down on an animated scene below with the chickens in the foreground adding a pleasing domestic touch. The engraving comes from John Britton's *Picturesque Antiquities of the English Cities* (140x195).

Two further views of the courtyard of the New Inn. Above is a drawing by E. J. Burrow from H. J. L. J. Masse's *Cathedral Church of Gloucester* of 1898 (100x110). Below is a view of the 1920s by A. Ward from his *Sketches of Gloucester* (90x100).

Elaborate carving on a beam at the New Inn. Above is a sketch by E. J. Burrow from H. J. L. J. Masse's *Cathedral Church of Gloucester* of 1898 (95x60). Below is a drawing by Frederick William Fairholt engraved by C. D. Laing from the *Builder* of 14 November 1846 (170x80).

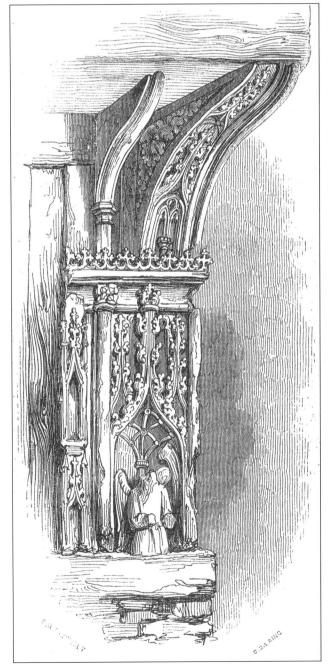

· ST. MARY'S STREET ·

Above is a view of St Mary's Street with the truncated spire of St Nicholas Church peeping over the rooftops (95x105) and below an entrance to the Little Cloister built against the east end of the Abbey refectory or frater and now part of a fifteent-century timber-framed house (130x65). Both drawings of the early 1920s are by A. Ward from his *Sketches of Gloucester.*

· LITTLE CLOISTERS ·

The Raven Tavern in Hare Lane, which was built in the sixteenth century and even at one time was important enough to issue its own token coinage. H. F. Trew restored the timber framed section in 1950 as an old people's club. This drawing by A. Ward of the 1920s comes from his *Sketches of Gloucester* (125x75).

The former Bell Inn in Southgate Street was demolished in 1968. It dated from at least 1544 and was the birthplace of George Whitefield, the famous eighteenth century non-conformist divine. From the 1830s onwards it became one of the important social centres of the City and was a focal point of the Conservative cause. This sketch of 1900 showing it with artistic licence in the eighteenth century comes from Albert Belden's *George Whitefield – The Awakener* of 1953 (155x90).

Number 154 Westgate Street, a sketch by F. W. Waller of 1877. It comes from volume two of the *Transactions of the Bristol and Gloucestershire Archaeological Society* of 1877/1878 (170x270).

A drawing of a medieval house in Gloucester by E. J. Burrow from H. J. L. J. Masse's *Cathedral Church of Gloucester* of 1898 (140x65).

Robert Raikes was one of the pioneers of Sunday Schools in this country. A view of one of the first Sunday Schools that was situated in Brunswick Road. A drawing of the 1920s by A. Ward from his *Sketches of Gloucester* (130x105).

- THE FIRST SUNDAY SCHOOL •

Numbers 36 and 38 Southgate Street form a very fine late sixteenth century timber framed house where Robert Raikes lived from 1768 to 1801. Above is a view by E. J. Burrow from H. L. J. L. Masse's *Cathedral Church of Gloucester* of 1898 (90x75) and below a drawing of the early 1920s by A. Ward from his *Sketches of Gloucester* (95x100).

Bishop Hooper was imprisoned in this house in Westgate Street the night before he was burnt at the stake as a Protestant heretic outside St Mary's Gate on 9 February 1555. Above is an etching of the house by Harold F. Trew in the *Builder* of 8 January 1915 (100x75) and below a sketch of the house by Fred Roe from P. H. Ditchfield's *Vanishing Britain* of 1910 (115x115).

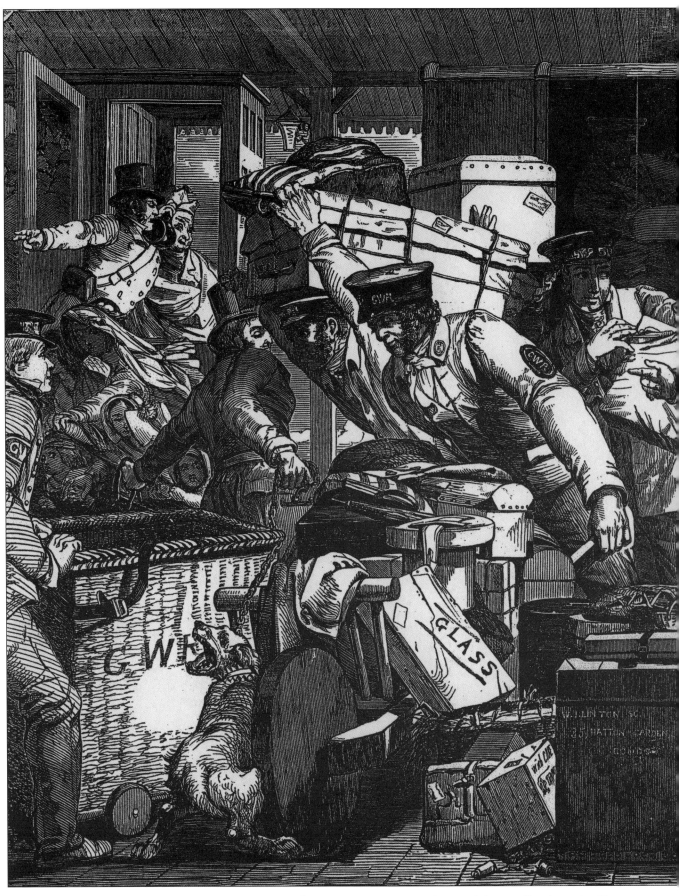

In the 1840s the differing railway gauges between the Great Western at 7 feet and the Midland at 4′ 8½″ were a cause of great frustration for travellers at Gloucester station where the two systems met. The *Illustrated London News* had a field day in 1846 when it sent one of its artists to the City and captured the scene of chaos abounding in the change over for its edition of 6 June. The break in the gauge lasted until 1854 (235x360).

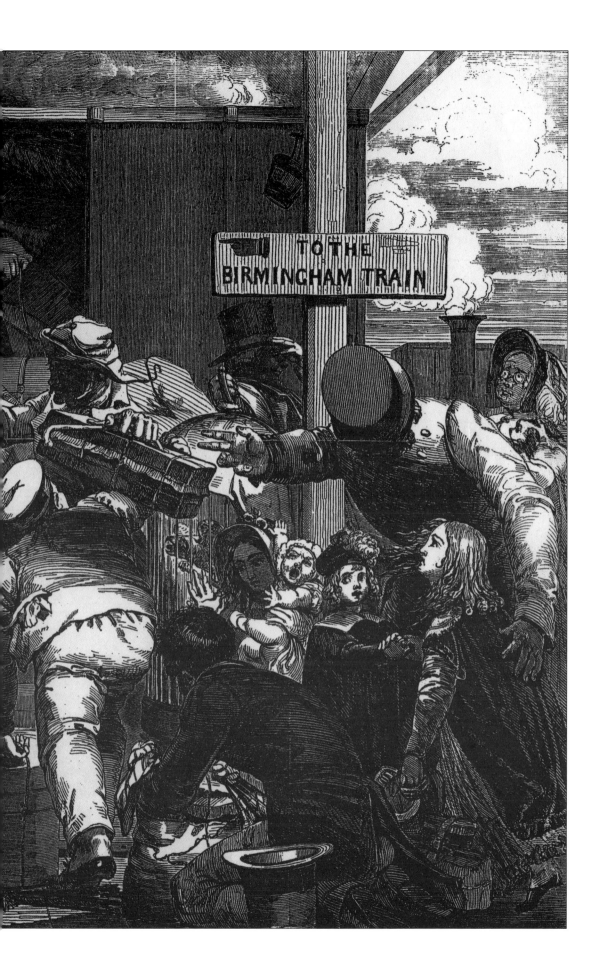

Two further anonymous views from the *Illustrated London News* of 6 June 1846 of the chaos caused by the changing of the gauge at Gloucester Station. Above the trans-shipment of goods (150x240) and below difficulty with horses (175x240).

A royal journey through the Midlands by train. Above is a view of the train passing through Cheltenham Station without stopping (150x230) and below the arrival at Gloucester for the change of trains necessitated by the break in the gauge (155x240). Incredible deference was shown with vast crowds, bells rung, salutes fired and loyal addresses presented. Both anonymous engravings are from the *Illustrated London News* of 6 October 1849.

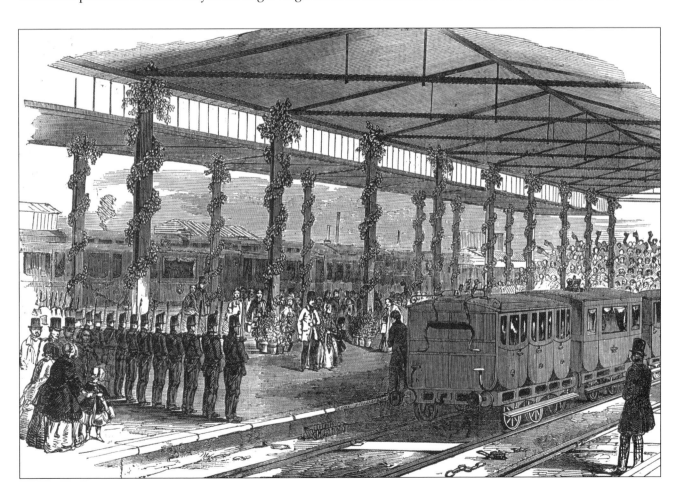

The anonymous engraving from the *Illustrated London News* of 27 April 1867 showing the great crowds present at the Docks for the launching of a lifeboat paid for by local public subscription (105x240).

A powerful sketch of the Docks in 1887 showing sailing vessels and a Severn trow. It is by Joseph Pennell from Mrs Schuyler Van Rensselaer's *English Cathedrals* of the same year (100x135).

THE CATHEDRAL

The story of the Cathedral is an intriguing one that goes back over thirteen hundred years to about 679 when king Osric founded a religious house in Gloucester dedicated to St Peter. This seems to have been set up originally as a nunnery for women of high birth with monks and clerks attached for liturgical purposes and the necessary manual work. The first Abbess was Kyneburga from the royal family of the Hwicce and there would have been enough personal servants to allow the nuns to live in the aristocratic style they had been used to from birth.

Bede, who lived about 673 to 735 complained that the high ideals of monasticism envisaged by the original founders of religious houses had been quietly forgotten and instead a life of considerable luxury had been substituted. Some ninety years after the original foundation during hostilities between King Egbert and the King of Mercia, the nuns were forcibly ejected and the buildings became ruinous. Some fifty years later they repaired and handed over to secular priests, a situation that seems to have lasted for a further two hundred and fifty years until 1022 or slightly earlier. About that time Benedictine rule was introduced by the Bishop of Worcester and the church had rebuilding work in 1058.

However it was the impetus provided by the arrival of Serlo the first Norman Abbot that really changed the situation. He had been a chaplain to the Conqueror and this influence in high places coupled with his own considerable powers set the Abbey on a new and energetic course of development. The number of monks increased steadily and a fire of 1088 gave Serlo the opportunity to rebuild the church on a scale he thought fitting. By 1100 enough of the eastern half of the building was completed to allow it to be consecrated and in 1121 for a second consecration to follow for the nave. The next year a fire is thought to have destroyed the wooden roof of the nave and during the rest of the twelfth century building work continued round the cloister area to the north. During this time the Abbey acquired vast territorial possessions and endowments and by 1216 it was considered important enough for the nine-year-old Henry III to be crowned in the church. By 1222 the central tower was rebuilt and by 1242 the stone vaulting of the nave was completed.

By 1318 remedial work had to be carried out by Abbot Thoky in the south aisle of the nave, which showed signs of collapsing and it was also revaulted. It is to this Decorated period that the lovely ballflower in the south aisle and chapels and triforium of the choir belong. The courage of Abbot Thoky was also to usher in a period of great prosperity for the Abbey, as

he sent his own escort to bring the body of the murdered Edward II from Berkeley castle for burial at Gloucester, where it became at once an object of veneration and pilgrimage. Edward's sumptuous tomb is one of the finest in the country and the donations and offerings were so great that they financed further extensive building work. The south transept was transformed and the choir remodelled to be followed by the north transept. This all took place between the 1330s and 1370s, now of course in the Perpendicular style, which may have been strongly influenced by the chapter house at old St Paul's and St Stephen's chapel in Westminster, but took on a character wholly its own.

The Perpendicular style progressed in the fifteenth century when Abbot Morwent rebuilt the west front and two westernmost bays of the nave and the south porch, which was heavily restored in the nineteenth century. In the 1450s during Abbot Seabroke's tenure of office, a monk named Robert Tully was responsible for the present central tower, which replaced the earlier structure and is now such an outstanding feature of the building. The last great achievement before the Dissolution was the rebuilding of the Lady Chapel between 1450 and 1500.

After the Dissolution the building had its narrowest squeak when its total destruction was planned during the Commonwealth, but in 1657 it was saved by the mayor and citizens. In the eighteenth century Bishop Martin Benson spent vast sums on restoration and in the nineteenth century there was extensive work by G. G. Scott including a new reredos. From 1953 onwards major roofing repairs became necessary for the nave, choir, north transept and cloisters.

However before considering the interior of the present Cathedral mention of course must be made of one of the great glories of the building, which is the set of cloisters with the earliest known fan vaulting in the country. In the north walk the original lavatorium or washing place for the monks still survives.

The interior has choir stalls of the 1370s with a wonderful collection of misericords, well augmented in the nineteenth century. The great east window of about 1350 was restored in the nineteenth and early twentieth centuries and is filled with a splendid collection of medieval stained glass. Elsewhere in the Cathedral, while there is other medieval glass, the rest of the story is largely Victorian with work by Kempe, Clayton and Bell and one or two others.

There are a large number of fine monuments in the Cathedral, the most outstanding being the already mentioned tomb of Edward II. Various abbots and bishops are commemorated in this way and two of the finest of the rest are the seventeenth century memorials to Alderman Blackleech and his wife and John Machen and his family.

Not many cathedrals in this country have such a fine setting and Gloucester with its position in a surrounding pastoral landscape can be seen in long perspective from a number of view points. Few perhaps seeing its distant central tower rising proudly above the surrounding rooftops can realise how miraculously it has survived the vicissitudes of a long and turbulent history.

A sketch by Herbert Railton of the tower of the Cathedral from *Dreamland in History – the Story of the Norman Dukes* of 1891 by H. D. M. Spence. It is a view from the south east along the length of Oxbody Lane, which was widened and truncated in the 1920s and is currently called the Oxbode (175x115).

A highly detailed drawing by Herbert Railton showing the central tower of the Cathedral from the west over rooftops. It also comes from *Dreamland in History – the Story of the Norman Dukes* of 1891 by H. D. M. Spence (170x125).

· CATHEDRAL TOWER ·

The central tower of the Cathedral drawn by A. Ward from his undated *Sketches of Gloucester*, which appears to be of the early 1920s (140x70).

The central tower of the Cathedral from the east The drawing is by E. J. Burrow of 1894 and comes from H. J. L. J. Masse's *Cathedral Church of Gloucester* of 1898 (100x60).

The central tower of the Cathedral as depicted by the architect W. Curtis Green. It comes from the *Builder* of 14 August 1909 for which periodical he produced a wide range of beautifully detailed drawings over a number of years (165x85).

As well as practising as an architect William Henry Bidlake was an excellent architectural draughtsman. At the age of twenty-one he won the R.I.B.A. silver medal for drawings in 1883 and the Pugin travelling studentship in 1885 (see also page 64 for his drawing of the south porch of the Cathedral). From 1919 to 1922 he was Director of the Birmingham School of Architecture and it is not hard to see from this youthful drawing why he had such success in later life. The illustration makes an interesting contrast with that on the previous page and comes from the *Builder* of 31 July 1886 (270x180).

A north-easterly view of the Cathedral from an engraving by James Sargant Storer after a drawing by his son Henry. It comes from James Sargant Storer's *History and Antiquities of the Cathedral Churches of Great Britain* of 1814 to 1819. This particular view is dated 1 December 1814 and the three figures give scale to the building (110x87).

This north-easterly view of the Cathedral dated 20 December 1828 is the first of a number of copper engravings in this work from John Britton's *Cathedral Antiquities*. This process gives a particularly soft and mellow reproduction and the engraver of this view is Henry Le Keux after a drawing by William Henry Bartlett. Two well dressed figures promenade on the lawn while the gardener sweeps up leaves. The roller in the foreground makes a pleasing horticultural detail (155x220).

A north-east view of the Cathedral by Alfred J. Dunn. It comes from volume one of the Architectural Association's Third Series of Sketch Books of 1893 (385x250).

Herbert Railton's sketch of College Lane with the entrance into the south east corner of College Green through College Court. The central tower of the Cathedral looms over this view which comes from *Dreamland in History – the Story of the Norman Dukes* of 1891 by the then Dean of Gloucester, H. D. M. Spence (135x75).

The Cathedral from the north east, a further sketch by Herbert Railton from *Dreamland in History – the Story of the Norman Dukes* by Dean Spence (150x120).

A view of the Cathedral from the south east by Orlando Jewitt, who in addition to being the artist also produced the wood engraving. It comes from Richard John King's *Handbook to the Cathedrals of England* of 1865 (145x100).

A high angle south-east view of the Cathedral by Joseph Pennell drawn from the tower of St John's Church on 21 June 1887. It comes from *English Cathedrals* by Mrs Schuyler Van Rensselaer, also of 1887 (135x130).

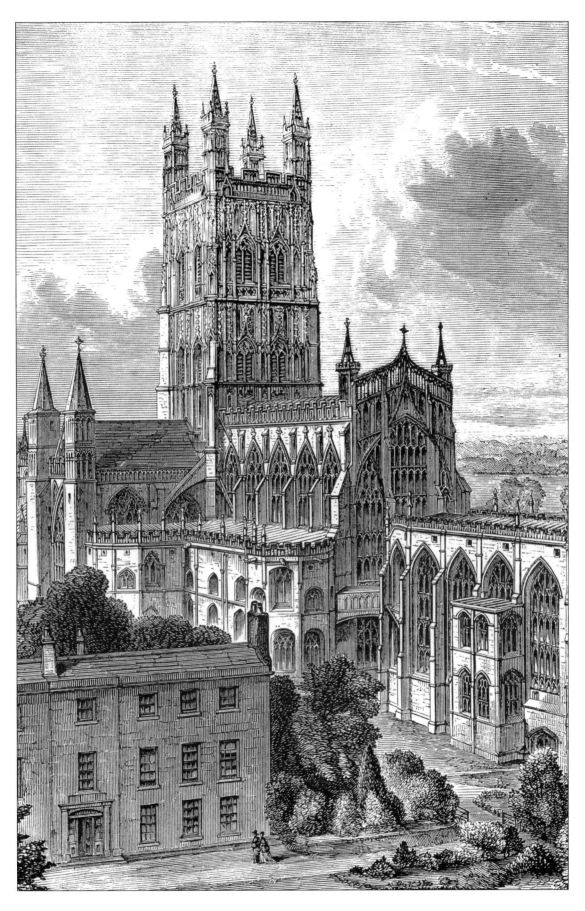

This anonymous wood engraving of the Cathedral from the southeast comes from volume two of *Our National Cathedrals* of 1888. This work is based on H. and B. *Winkles' Cathedral Churches of England and Wales* of 1836 to 1842, but has further illustrations and additional material about restorations during the intervening years between the two publications (180x125).

A south-eastern view of the Cathedral through the foliage of high summer. The artist is Herbert Railton and the drawing comes from *Dreamland in History – the Story of the Norman Dukes* of 1891 by the then Dean of Gloucester, H. D. M. Spence (130x110).

A. Ward's drawing of a south eastern view of the cathedral from his undated *Sketches of Gloucester* (125x120).

A view of the south transept and central tower of the Cathedral dated 1 May 1829. A woman and child and another figure about to disappear into the passageway on the right give scale to the building on a cloudy spring day. The artist is William Henry Bartlett and the engraver is John Le Keux and the view comes from John Britton's *Cathedral Antiquities* (220x170).

Another illustration from John Britton's *Cathedral Antiquities*, which is dated 1 November 1828. it shows a half elevation and half section of the tower and transept of the cathedral. The letter D above the roof line to the right of the tower denotes that this is the south transept. The drawing made in 1827 is by H. Ansted and the engraver is John Le Keux (230x160).

The Cathedral from the cloisters drawn by Charles Edward Mallows, who trained as an architect, but spent most of his working life as a draughtsman of highly detailed drawings. Mallows was a great friend of Joseph Pennell and they often sketched together. On one occasion they were so engrossed in drawing the Galilee in Durham Cathedral that they were locked in by mistake. They were totally unfazed by this occurence and pulled with a will on the bell ropes, which brought everybody running, much to their amusement. This view comes from the *Builder* of 5 December 1891 (385x280).

A view of the north transept of the Cathedral seen from the cloisters dated 1 December 1814. The artist and engraver is James Sargant Storer and it comes from his *History and Antiquities of the Cathedral Churches of Great Britain* of 1814 to 1819 (120x87).

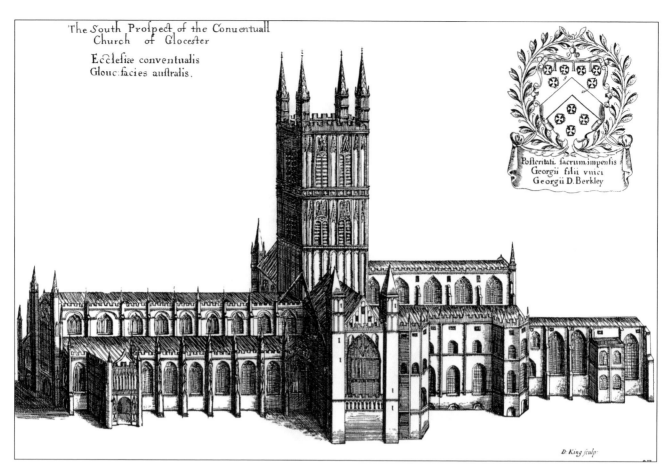

The South Prospect of the Conuentuall
Church of Glocester

Ecclefiæ conventualis
Glouc.facies auftralis.

Pofteritati. facrum.impenfis
Georgii filii vnici
Georgii D.Berkley

D. King sculp.

A south view of the cathedral, which appeared originally in Sir William Dugdale's *Monasticon Anglicanum* published between 1655 and 1673. The artist is Richard Newcourt and the engraver Daniel King, who is thought to have died in 1664. The latter published a selection from the *Monasticon* in 1656 under the title *Cathedrall and Conventuall Churches of England and Wales*. King's engravings are fairly crude, but nevertheless they give an early record of architectural features which were later modified. Dugdale had a poor opinion of King and called him 'an ignorant silly fellow, an arrant knave' (185x280).

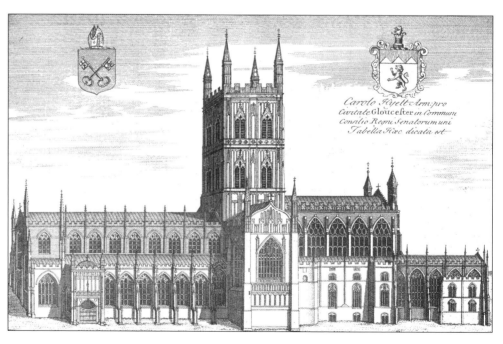

Carolo Hyett Arm.pro
Civitate Gloucester in Communi
Consilio Regni Senatorumuni
Tabella Hæc dicata est

A view entitled 'South Prospect of the Cathedral Church of St Peter at Gloucester'
engraved by John Harris for Browne Willis' *Survey of Cathedrals* of 1727 (170x270).

A south view of the Cathedral by John Harris (a different person from the John Harris on the previous page) included in Francis Grose's *Antiquities of England and Wales* published between 1773 and 1787 (140x185).

A drawing of the Cathedral from the south west dated 1 November 1819 by John Chessel Buckler from his *Views of Cathedral Churches in England and Wales* of 1822 (165x245).

A view of the Cathedral from the south west dated
1 December 1828. The artist is William Henry Bartlett
and the engraver Robert Sands and the work comes
from John Britton's *Cathedral Antiquities*. A number of
people shown in the vicinity of the south porch are
possibly gathering for a service of some kind
(150x215).

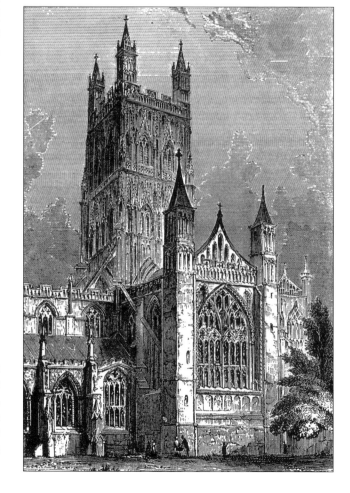

The south transept and tower of the Cathedral figure
prominently in this anonymous view from the
Reverend Jabez Marrat's undated *Our Sea-Girt Isle*,
one of the many mid-Victorian works which extol the
virtues of a smiling countryside and quickly pass over
the misery of working class areas in large cities
(132x90).

The south side of the Cathedral from a drawing by Frederick Nash engraved by James Sargant Storer. It comes from the Gloucestershire volume of the *Beauties of England and Wales*, the enormous series covering the country by counties, which was published between 1810 and 1818 (100x155).

A later view of the south side of the Cathedral showing Victorian alterations to the south porch. It comes from the Reverend H. H. Bishop's *Pictorial Architecture of the British Isles* of 1890 (105x140).

Samuel Rawle is the engraver of this 1798 view of the south porch of the cathedral which comes from Thomas Dudley Fosbroke's *Original History of the City of Gloucester* of 1819 (180x125).

A mother and presumably her daughter pause in front of the south porch of the Cathedral in this view drawn and engraved by John Sargant Storer. It comes from his *History and Antiquities of the Cathedral Churches of Great Britain* and is dated 1 December 1814 (115x87).

The south porch of the Cathedral drawn by William Henry Bartlett and engraved by John Le Keux. This highly detailed view dated 1 July 1828 comes from John Britton's *Cathedral Antiquities* (220x165).

The Three Choirs Festival of Gloucester, Hereford and Worcester seems to have been started as early as the second decade of the eighteenth century. This anonymous engraving from the *Illustrated London News* dated 14 September 1850 shows carriages at the south porch of the Cathedral depositing fashionable members of the audience for a concert (110x150).

Crowds gathering for a Three Choirs Festival concert at the south porch of the Cathedral where an entrance canopy has been provided, presumably to give some protection from bad weather. This anonymous engraving also comes from the *Illustrated London News* at the later date of 23 September 1865 (152x115).

This beautifully detailed drawing of the south porch of the Cathedral dated 12 July 1884 by William Henry Bidlake helped him to win the Pugin Travelling Scholarship for 1885 (see also page 43 for his drawing of the central tower of the Cathedral) (270x180).

The south porch of the Cathedral after the renovations by Francis Redfern as drawn by E. Senior and engraved by one of the Whymper family for *Picturesque Europe*. This work is undated but appears to be of the 1880s (175x155).

Two views of the Cathedral by Thomas Hearne from his *Antiquities of Great Britain*. The north-west view above is an engraving by William Byrne dated 15 April 1797 while the south-west view below dated 12 April 1806 is by William's son John a year after William's own death. The *Antiquities* was issued originally in parts and then in two volumes, the first from 1778 to 1786 and the second from 1797 to 1806 (above 185x255 below 185x250).

Joseph Pennell chose the high view point of the tower of St Mary de Lode for his sketch of the Cathedral from the north west. It comes from Mrs Schuyler Van Rensselaer's *English Cathedrals* of 1887 (120x125).

The west front of the Cathedral from an engraving by James Sargant Storer after a drawing by his son Henry. It comes from James Sargant Storer's *History and Antiquities by the Cathedral Churches of Great Britain* of 1814 to 1819. This particular view is dated 1 December 1814 (120x87).

A section through the second compartment from the west end of the Cathedral drawn by H. Ansted in October 1826 and engraved by Henry Le Keux. The engraving is dated 1 March 1828 and it comes from John Britton's *Cathedral Antiquities* (160x225).

The west front of the Cathedral drawn by William Henry Bartlett and engraved by William Woolnoth. People are going into the Cathedral on a cloudy day in high summer and two figures in the best half-hearted traditions of the British workman are digging on the right under the tree. The engraving also comes from John Britton's *Cathedral Antiquities* and is dated 1 November 1828 (170x220).

The west front and south side of the Cathedral drawn by William Warren and engraved by B. Winkles. The view comes from the H. and B. Winkles' *Cathedral Churches of England and Wales* of 1836 to 1842 with a text by Thomas Moule, who is better known for his cartographic work (108x140).

The Cathedral seen from the north west across rooftops by Herbert Railton in *Dreamland in History – The Story of the Norman Dukes* of 1891 by H. D. M. Spence. The viewpoint is very similar, but not so high, as that of Joseph Pennell on page 67 (175x125).

Two bays of the nave on the south side of the Cathedral, a drawing made by Sidney K. Greenslade during an Architectural Association excursion of 1895. It comes from the *Builder* of 24 August 1895 (260x182).

A view of part of the interior of the nave featuring the elegant screen by William Kent of 1741. A replacement designed by Robert Smirke was in position by 1832, several years after this 1816 illustration drawn and engraved by James Sargant Storer for his *History and Antiquities of the Cathedral Churches of Great Britain* (112x87).

The nave as seen by Herbert Railton in *Dreamland in History – the Story of Norman Dukes* of 1891 by H. M. D. Spence. It shows Robert Smirke's screen clearly as a prominent feature of this view down the nave (100x110).

A view down the nave looking towards the choir by Joseph Pennell from Mrs Schuyler Van Rensselaer's *English Cathedrals* of 1887. The engraver is R. C. Collins (95x105).

The very elegant doorway leading out of the nave engraved by James Sargant Storer after a drawing by his son Henry. It comes from James Sargant Storer's *History and Antiquities of the Cathedral Churches of Great Britain* of 1814 to 1819. This particular engraving is dated 1 December 1814 (120x82).

The nave of the Cathedral looking towards the choir in a drawing dated 1 May 1829 by William Henry Bartlett engraved by William Woolnoth. It comes from John Britton's *Cathedral Antiquities* and includes a great deal of activity. On the right beside one of the pillars a group of people are talking, a rather disorganised group of choir boys are processing behind a cleric and there are sundry visitors looking around the building (205x165).

This anonymous engraving from the *Illustrated London News* of 14 September 1850 shows a Three Choirs Festival performance taking place in the Cathedral (235x180).

A performance of the Three Choirs Festival taking place in the Cathedral nave in 1865. The view is from an anonymous engraving in the *Illustrated London News* of 23 September of the same year (350x240).

A further performance at a Three Choirs Festival, but with no specific date. It comes from *Our National Cathedrals* of 1888 (150x100).

The west end of the Cathedral nave drawn and engraved by Orlando Jewitt for Richard John King's *Handbook to the Cathedrals of England* of 1865 with visitors discussing and admiring architectural features of the building (140x90).

A powerful drawing of part of the nave by Charles Edward Mallows. It comes from the *Builder* of 5 December 1891 (390x250).

Part of the nave as seen from the north aisle of the Cathedral by Joseph Pennell in Mrs Schuyler Van Rensselaer's *English Cathedrals* of 1887. The engraver is H. E. Sylvester (140x112).

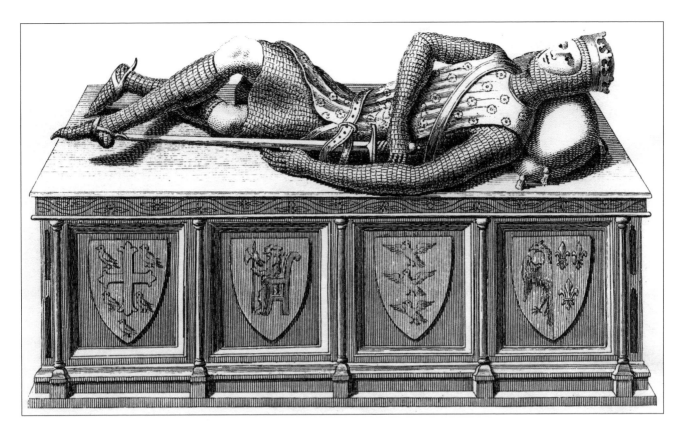

The effigy of Robert Curthose, Duke of Normandy and eldest son of the Conqueror, which rests on a wooden tomb of the fourteenth or fifteenth century in the centre of the cathedral presbytery. The effigy itself is made of Irish bog oak and probably of the mid thirteenth century. It suffered considerable damage during the Civil War, but was repaired at the Restoration. The anonymous engraving above is from Thomas Dudley Fosbroke's *Original History of the City of Gloucester* of 1819 (105x180). The artist and engraver of the illustration below is Orlando Jewitt and it comes from Richard John King's *Handbook to the Cathedrals of England* of 1865 (105x180).

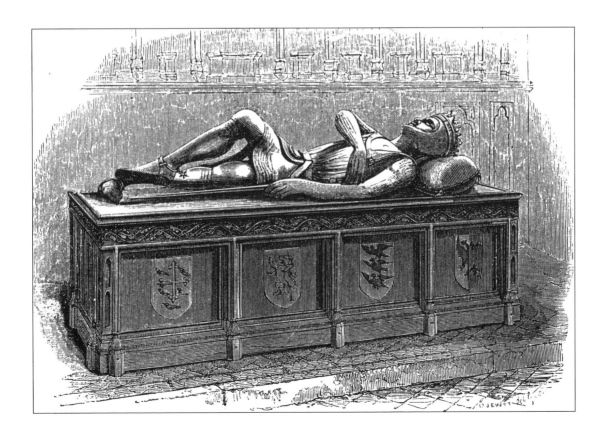

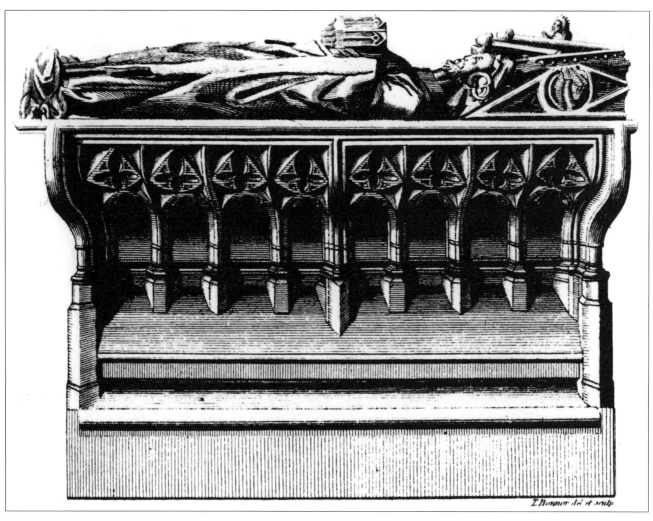

This bracket monument with a thirteenth century effigy was thought originally to represent Aldred, Bishop of Worcester, who has been credited by some authorities as having built a new church for St Peter's Abbey in 1056. It is now thought more likely that the effigy is actually that of Abbot Serlo, the first Norman abbot, and it stands on the south side of the Cathedral presbytery. The illustration above drawn and engraved by Thomas Bonnor comes from Thomas Dudley Fosbroke's *Original History of the City of Gloucester* of 1819 (90x125) while that below is engraved by Thomas Williams from a drawing of 1829 by William Henry Bartlett in John Britton's *Cathedral Antiquities* (70x110).

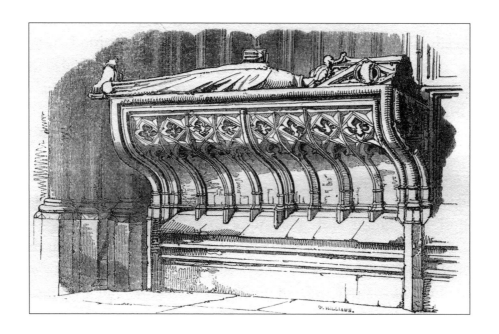

The monument to Ralph Bigland, Garter Principal King of Arms (1711-1784) in the north aisle of the Cathedral. The artist is simply called Ross and the engraver is Joseph Lee. The illustration comes from Thomas Dudley Fosbroke's *Original History of the City of Gloucester* of 1819. Bigland is noted for having produced a two volume work entitled *Historical, Monumental and Genealogical Collections Relative to the County of Gloucester* published in 1791 (280x140).

The memorial to Bishop Benson, which is situated in the north aisle of the Cathedral. Benson was Bishop from 1734 to 1752 and during his episcopate spent considerable sums on improvements to the palace, the repaving of the nave, the choir screen by William Kent and adorning parts of the exterior of the Cathedral with crocketed pinnacles. Thomas Bonnor is both the artist and engraver responsible for this representation of the memorial and it comes from Thomas Dudley Fosbroke's *Original History of the City of Gloucester* of 1819 (290x125).

The very elaborate monument to Christian and Thomas Machen in the north aisle of the Cathedral. Machen was three times Mayor of Gloucester during the sixteenth century and obviously a man of considerable importance. Thomas and his wife, who were married for fifty years, face each other across reading desks with the figure of Time above them carrying a broken scythe and hour glass as a *memento mori*. Beneath are ranged in neat order their seven sons and six daughters. Thomas Bonnor is the artist and engraver responsible for the representation of the monument and it is included in Thomas Dudley Fosbroke's *Original History of the City of Gloucester* of 1819 (195x170).

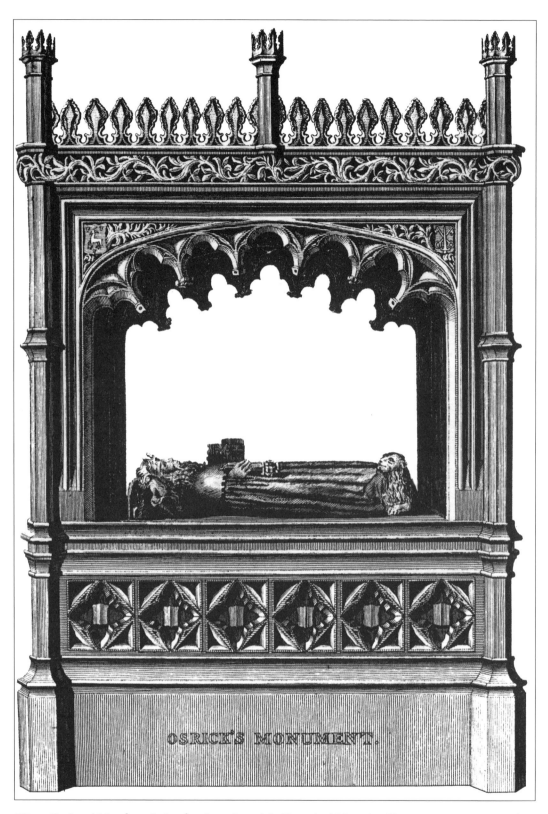

OSRICK'S MONUMENT.

King Osric of Northumbria, the founder of St Peter's Abbey in Gloucester was given this monument by Abbot Parker during the latter's period of office from 1514 to 1539. The tomb now stands in the north ambulatory of the Cathedral and Parker's own arms appear in the spandrels of the canopy. Osric holds a model of the Abbey in his left hand and is crowned and sceptred. Thomas Bonnor is the artist and engraver responsible for this representation of the monument, which comes from Thomas Dudley Fosbroke's *Original History of the City of Gloucester* of 1819 (220x155).

King Osric's monument as seen in an engraving by James Sargant Storer after a drawing by his son Henry. It comes from James Sargant Storer's *History and Antiquities of the Cathedral Churches of Great Britain* of 1814 to 1819. The date of this particular engraving is 1 December 1814 (120x82).

A representation of effigy on King Osric's monument drawn and engraved by G. F. Storm after a sketch by John Carter. It comes from John Britton's *Cathedral Antiquities* and is dated 1 November 1828 (140x50).

Two views of the monument of King Osric by Herbert Railton. Above is a view of the monument itself (145x80). Below is a representation of the monument in its wider setting (130x75). Both come from *Cloister Life in the Days of Coeur de Lion* of 1893 by H. D. M. Spence, the then Dean of Gloucester.

William Parker was the last Abbot of St Peter's Abbey before the Dissolution and died just before it was secularised. He thus avoided the indignity of having to see his life's work and the long history of the Abbey coming to an end. Parker built a chantry for himself beside the shrine of Edward II and had an impressive alabaster effigy made. However there is very great doubt whether he was actually interred in it. Thomas Bonnor is the artist and engraver of this view, which comes from Thomas Dudley Fosbroke's *Original History of the City of Gloucester* of 1819 (105x135).

Ambulatory showing Shrine of Edward II.

Herbert Railton

When Edward II was murdered in the most appalling fashion in Berkeley castle in 1327, nobody could be found initially brave enough to offer him a resting place. However Abbot Thoky of St Peter's Abbey sent his own carriage and retinue to the Castle and brought him back for burial. He now rests in one of the most sumptuous tombs in all England of about 1330 in the north ambulatory of the Cathedral. From the Abbey's point of view the burial proved to be a piece of enlightened self-interest, as pilgrims flocked to venerate him and brought great riches to the foundation. This sketch by Herbert Railton comes from *Dreamland in History – the Story of the Norman Dukes* of 1891 by H. D. M. Spence (110x110).

The monument to Edward II in the north ambulatory of the Cathedral drawn and engraved by Thomas Bonnor for Thomas Dudley Fosbroke's *Original History of the City of Gloucester* of 1819 (240x140).

Edward II's monument in the north ambulatory of the Cathedral drawn in 1827 by H. Ansted and engraved by John Le Keux. The engraving is actually dated 1 July 1828 and comes from John Britton's *Cathedral Antiquities* (230x150).

Edward II was the founder of Oriel College, Oxford, which restored the canopy of the monument in the north ambulatory three times in the eighteenth century. The capitals of the adjoining columns were painted brown with a motif of white harts after a visit by Richard II in 1378. The artist of this view is John Willis and the engraver Joseph Skelton and it comes from the latter's *Pietas Oxoniensis* of 1828. The engraving itself is dated 1 May 1830 and is a good example of how copies of works held in sheets were released onto the market, but still retained original and earlier publication dates on title pages (270x190).

Another view of Edward II's monument drawn and engraved by Orlando Jewitt, which comes from Richard John King's *Handbook to the Cathedrals of England* of 1865 (145x97).

The effigy of Edward II which lies within his monument. It comes from John Britton's *Cathedral Antiquities* and is dated 1 November 1828. The artist and engraver is G. F. Storm 'from sketches by the late John Carter' (145x45).

Two views of the Cathedral triforium. The sketch above is by Gerald Horsley and comes from *The History of Gothic Art in England* by Edward Prior of 1899 (105x110) while that below is by A. Ward from his *Sketches of Gloucester* of the early 1920s (85x95).

The audience for a Three Choirs Festival concert in 1865 was so great some people had to listen from the triforium. This anonymous engraving comes from the *Illustrated London News* of 23 September 1865 (150x115).

The small chapel in the triforium, as seen in an anonymous engraving in Richard John King's *Handbook to the Cathedrals of England* of 1865 (70x80).

A view in the north transept of the Cathedral looking south west drawn by H. Ansted and engraved by John Le Keux. It is dated 1 April 1829 and comes from John Britton's *Cathedral Antiquities*. A procession of choir boys is forming up, while somebody behind probably in a hurry pauses to tie up a shoe lace (220x160).

The north transept of the Cathedral drawn by Benjamin Baud and engraved by B. Winkles. The view comes from H. and B. Winkles' *Cathedral Churches of England and Wales* of 1836 to 1842 with a text by Thomas Moule (145x105).

A drawing by William Henry Bartlett engraved by John Le Keux of the north transept looking north east in the Cathedral. The screen at the left with beautiful detailing is often called the reliquary and is a prominent feature of this view, which is dated April 1828 and comes from John Britton's *Cathedral Antiquities* (215x160).

The reliquary drawn and engraved by Orlando Jewitt for Richard John King's *Handbook to the Cathedrals of England* of 1865 (90x100).

A finely detailed drawing of the reliquary screen by Sidney K. Greenslade made during an *Architectural Association* sketching tour in 1895. It comes from the *Builder* of 24 August 1895 (260x185).

Above is the reliquary screen and below a view looking out of the north transept. Both sketches are by
Herbert Railton from *Dreamland in History – the Story of
the Norman Dukes* of 1891 by H. D. M. Spence (above
115x110 and below 125x70).

Abbot Seabroke held office from 1450 to 1457 and was buried in a chapel at the south-west end of the choir with an alabaster effigy placed on an altar tomb. The chapel used to be known as the Salutation of the Blessed Virgin Mary, but is generally named Seabroke's Chapel today. The drawing and engraving by Thomas Bonnor come from Thomas Dudley Fosbroke's *Original History of the City of Gloucester* of 1819 (72x135).

Alderman Abraham Blackleech, who died in 1639, and his wife Gertrude are represented by the two fine recumbent effigies on a tomb chest in the south transept of the Cathedral. Various guesses have been made as to the artist responsible, but no firm evidence has been found. Thomas Bonnor is the artist and engraver of this view of the effigies and it is perhaps a little unfortunate that he has given them a slightly furtive and shifty air. The engraving comes from Thomas Dudley Fosbroke's *Original History of the City of Gloucester* of 1819 (185x115).

John Jones was three times Mayor of Gloucester, a Member of Parliament for the City at the time of the Gunpowder Plot and a registrar to no less than eight bishops. He was meticulous in his duties and before his death commissioned his own monument, now on the west wall of the south aisle of the Cathedral. The monument was finished on 30 May 1630 and having already paid the craftsmen, Jones proceeded to die two days later on 1 June. The drawing and engraving are by Thomas Bonnor and come from Thomas Dudley Fosbroke's *Original History of the City of Gloucester* of 1819 (125x70).

The elegant monument to Lady Strachan, who died in 1770, is by Ricketts of Gloucester. It is situated in the south aisle of the Cathedral and a cherub holds Lady Strachan's portrait in a medallion. The drawing and engraving by Thomas Bonnor also come from Thomas Dudley Fosbroke's *Original History of the City of Gloucester* of 1819 (150x75).

A view looking east into the south aisle of the choir in the Cathedral with a workman lighting the way into the crypt from its entrance. The drawing is by William Henry Bartlett and the engraver John Le Keux. It is dated April 1828 and comes from John Britton's *Cathedral Antiquities* (210x160).

An almost exact replica of the engraving on the previous page, but without the workman. The artist is Herbert Railton and the sketch comes from *Dreamland in History – the Story of the Norman Dukes* of 1891 by the then Dean of Gloucester, H. D. M. Spence (135x90).

This view of the Cathedral crypt looking east comes from an engraving dated 1 May 1829 when it was still full of rubbish and acting as a charnel house, a situation not changed until 1851. The drawing is by William Henry Bartlett and engraved by John Le Keux for John Britton's *Cathedral Antiquities* (160x215).

Two views of the Cathedral crypt. That above is anonymous and comes from Richard John King's *Handbook to the Cathedrals of England* of 1865 (70x75). The one below is by A. Ward of the early 1920s from his *Sketches of Gloucester* (85x110).

Two further views of the Cathedral crypt. That above comes from the *Builder* of 15 November 1856 and is by Frederick S. Waller, Architect to the Cathedral from 1878 to 1905 (70x80). The one below is by Hugh Thomson of 1919 and comes from *Highways and Byways in Gloucestershire* by Edward Hutton, published in 1932 twelve years after Thomson's death (90x90).

Three compartments on the north side of the Cathedral choir. The artist is H. Ansted and the engraver John Le Keux and the view is dated 1 March 1828. It comes from John Britton's *Cathedral Antiquities* (230x145).

A view of the Cathedral choir looking east drawn in 1827 by H. Ansted. The engraving is by John Le Keux and dated 1 July 1828. It also comes from John Britton's *Cathedral Antiquities* (230x160).

A representation of the Cathedral choir looking towards the great east window before Sir George Gilbert Scott's restoration of 1867 onwards. The drawing and engraving are by Orlando Jewitt for Richard John King's *Handbook to the Cathedrals of England* of 1865 (150x98).

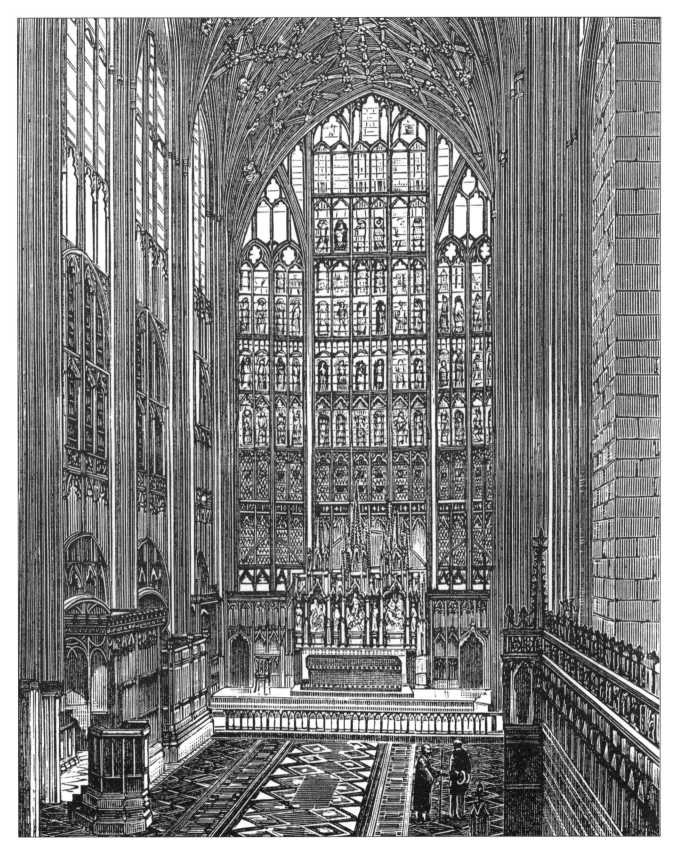

The Cathedral choir after Sir George Gilbert Scott's restoration of 1867 onwards. This anonymous engraving comes from *Our National Cathedrals* of 1888 (125x100).

Charles Edward Mallows beautifully detailed view of the Cathedral choir looking towards the great east window. It comes from the *Builder* of 5 December 1891 (390x270).

112

A similar view point to the drawing on the previous page looking towards the great east window. This sketch of 1919 by Hugh Thomson was not published until twelve years after his death when it appeared in *Highways & Byways in Gloucestershire* by Edward Hutton (135x90).

Sir George Gilbert Scott's new reredos for the Cathedral, an engraving with the artist distinguishing only by the initials J. M. W. It comes from the *Builder* of 22 February 1873. It would be interesting to know what Scott's reaction would have been, had he been alive today and seen the present polychroming of his work (275x175).

Armorial tiling in the Cathedral choir, which dates originally from the time of Abbot Seabroke (1450-1457). It was much restored and altered, especially in the nineteenth century. The drawing of part of the tiling comes from Thomas Dudley Fosbrooke's *Original History of the City of Gloucester* of 1819 and seems to be based on John Carter's work of some thirty years earlier (225x220).

John Carter's drawing of the armorial tiling in the Cathedral choir dated 1 May 1788. It comes from volume two of his *Specimens of Ancient Sculpture and Painting* of 1787 (225x390).

The east end of the Lady Chapel in the Cathedral
drawn by H. Ansted in 1827. The engraving dated 1
July is by William Woolnoth and comes from John
Britton's *Cathedral Antiquities* (220x160).

The Lady Chapel seen from the east end. The view above drawn and engraved by
Thomas Bonnor comes from Thomas Dudley's Fosbroke's *Original History of the City
of Gloucester* of 1819 (85x135). That below is drawn by Benjamin Baud and engraved
by B. Winkles in H. and B. Winkles' *Cathedral Churches of England and Wales* of 1836 to
1842 (140x108).

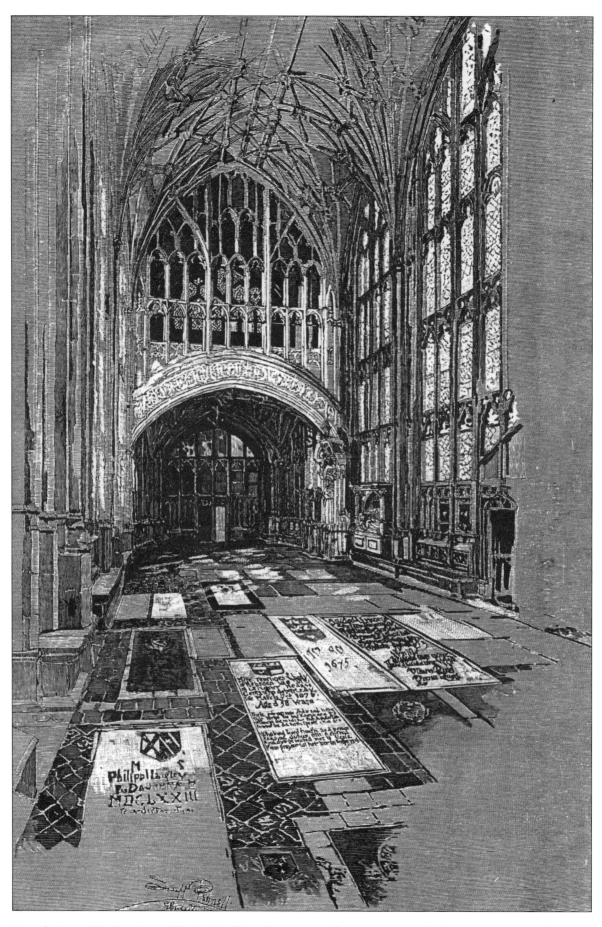

Joseph Pennell's drawing of the Lady Chapel seen from the east end, with the grave slabs on the floor given great prominence. The engraver is M. Jones and the view comes from Mrs Schuyler Van Rensselaer's *English Cathedrals* of 1887 (150x100).

Bishop Goldesborough's episcopate lasted from 1598 to 1604 and he is commemorated by a painted oolite efigy on an altar tomb in the Cathedral's Lady Chapel. This representation is drawn and engraved by Thomas Bonnor and appears in Thomas Dudley Fosbroke's *Original History of the City of Gloucester* of 1819 (100x125).

The Lady Chapel seen by Herbert Railton in *Dreamland in History – the Story of the Norman Dukes* of 1891 by H. D. M.Spence (140x125).

The very fine marble monument to Sir John Powell by Thomas Green of Camberwell in the Cathedral's Lady Chapel. Powell fell foul of James II, but returned to favour under William III. He was a Baron of the Exchequer and a judge in Common Pleas and from 1685 represented his native city of Gloucester in Parliament. He died in 1713 and Thomas Bonnor is the artist and engraver of this representation of the monument in Thomas Dudley Fosbroke's *Original History of the City of Gloucester* of 1819 (290x145).

Elizabeth Williams (neé Smith) and Margery Clent (also neé Smith) were daughters of Bishop Miles Smith, Bishop from 1612 to 1624. Elizabeth died in 1622 aged only seventeen and Margery in the following year. Both have excellent memorials by local craftsmen in the Lady Chapel. These were engraved by Thomas Bonnor for Thomas Dudley Fosbroke's *Original History of the City of Gloucester* of 1819 (Above Margery Clent 100x60 and below Elizabeth Williams 140x155).

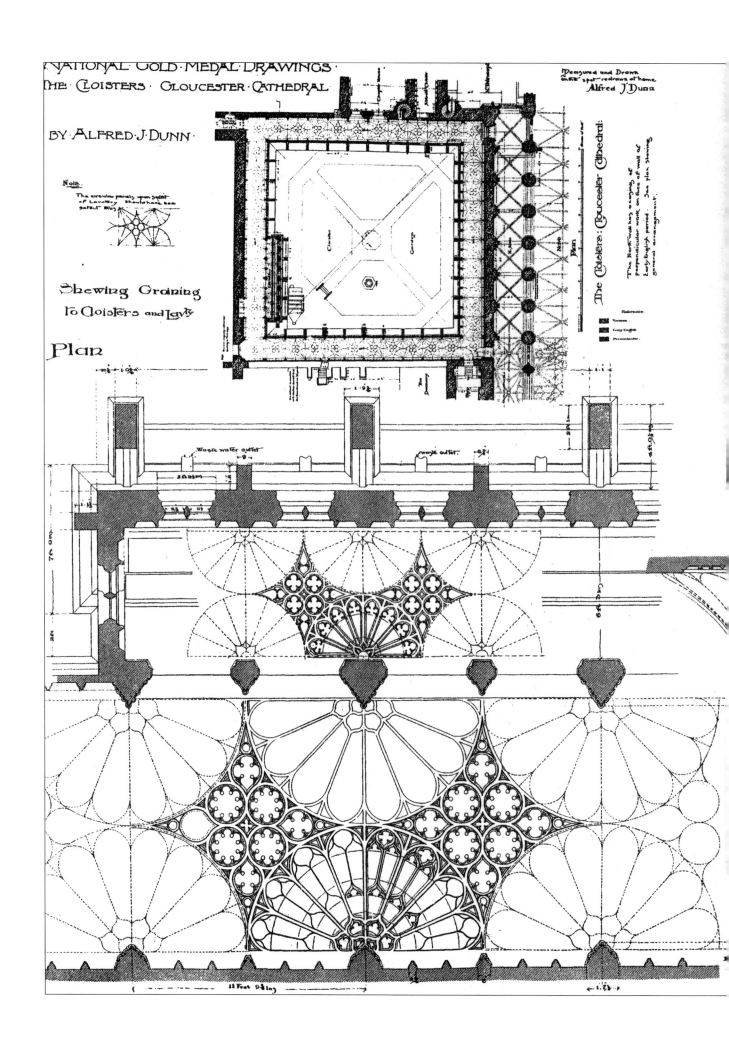

NATIONAL GOLD MEDAL DRAWINGS
THE CLOISTERS GLOUCESTER CATHEDRAL

BY ALFRED J DUNN

Measured and Drawn
on the spot redrawn at home
Alfred J Dunn

Note:

The circular panels upon front
of Lavatory should have been
perfect litty

Shewing Graining
to Cloisters and Lavy

Plan

The Cloisters: Gloucester Cathedral:

124

The Cathedral cloisters, built originally for St Peter's Abbey between the mid fourteenth and early fifteenth centuries, are one of the great glories of the building and contain the earliest remaining fan vaulting in the country. They have naturally attracted the attention of many artists and this series of measured drawings by Alfred J. Dunn comes from the *Building News* of 9 November 1894 (280x380).

of the Lavatory Arcade:
One Bay

of the Nth Wall:
One Bay

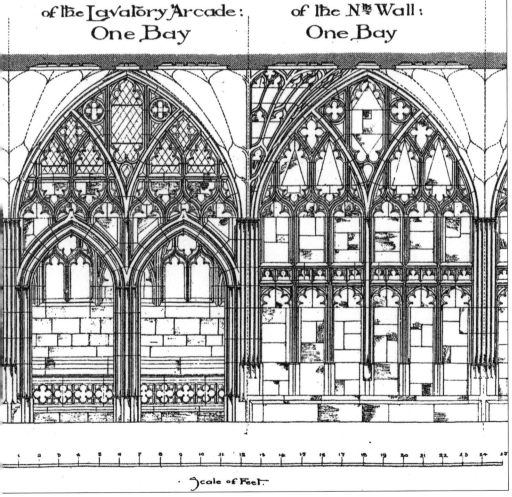

· Scale of Feet·

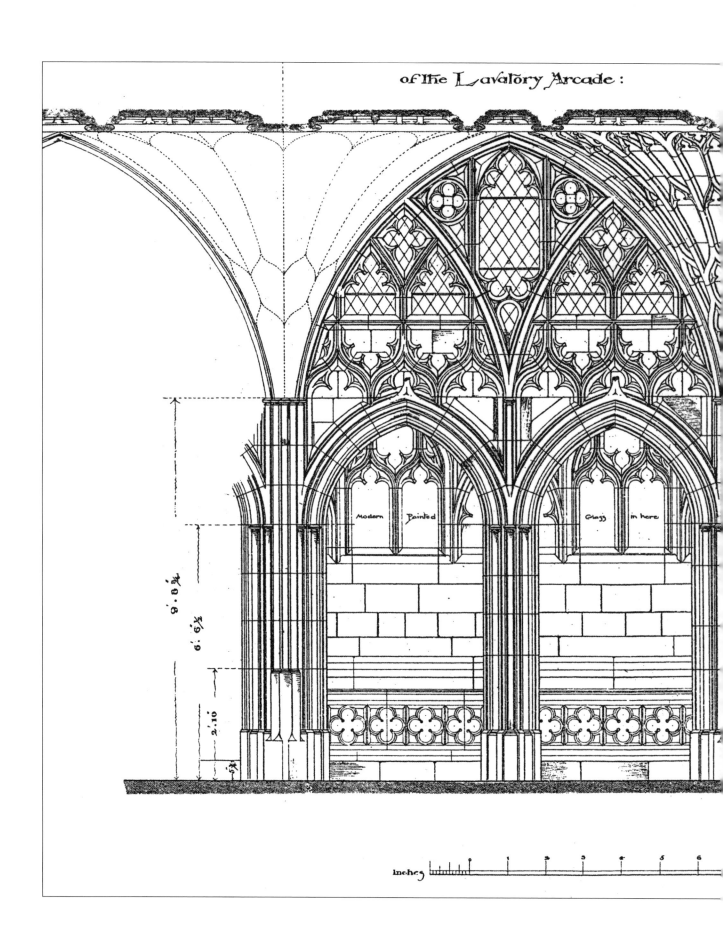

Modern   Painted   Glass   in here

Inches

A more detailed measured drawing of two bays of the north walk of the Cathedral cloisters showing the entrance to the monk's lavatorium or washing place. It is by Alfred J. Dunn from volume one of the Architectural Association's *Third Series of Sketch Books* of 1893 (255x340).

One of Charles Edward Mallows' splendid drawings showing the north walk of the cloisters with the monks' lavatorium or washing place. It comes from the *Builder* of 5 December 1891 (300x380).

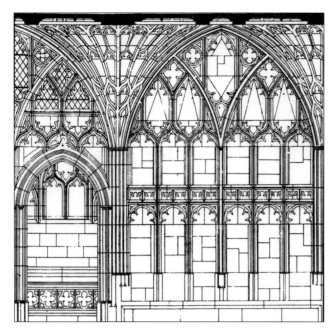

Gerald Horsley is the artist responsible for a bay of the north walk of the cloisters with the entrance to the monks' lavatorium or washing place. It comes from Edward Prior's *History of Gothic Art in England* of 1899 (112x112).

Part of the north walk of the cloisters and the entrance to the lavatorium by Herbert Railton from *Dreamland in History – the Story of the Norman Dukes* of 1891 by H. D. M. Spence (120x70).

A view showing fashionable people parading along the north walk of the cloisters. William Henry Bartlett is the artist responsible for the drawing, except for the people, who have been added by W. H. Brooke. The engraver of this work dated 1 December 1828 is John Le Keux and it comes from John Britton's *Cathedral Antiquities* (215x165).

Benjamin Baud is the artist of this view of the
Cathedral cloisters with two matronly figures and
their children admiring the vaulting. It is engraved by
B. Winkles for H. and B. Winkles' *Cathedral Churches of
England and Wales* of 1836 to 1842 (140x108).

The north aisle of the cloisters drawn and etched by Samuel Lysons for his quaintly named work *Etchings of Views and Antiquities in the County of Gloucester Hitherto Imperfectly or Never Engraved* of 1791 (380x260).

The Cloisters
Glo'ster Cath'l

134

A view of the south walk of the cloisters by Alfred J. Dunn dated September 1893, which comes from volume one of the Architectural Association's *Third Series o fSketch Books* (255x330).

W. Curtis Green as well as being a practising architect was also an excellent draughtsman and produced a great deal of detailed work for the *Builder* over a number of years. This view of the cloisters in fact comes from the *Builder* of 14 August 1909 (260x185).

The south walk of the cloisters showing the carrels where the monks could write and illuminate manuscripts. Orlando Jewitt is the artist responsible for drawing and engraving this view, which comes from Richard John King's *Handbook to the Cathedrals of England* of 1865 (135x97).

The north east corner of the cloisters as seen by the Japanese architect Kotaro Sakurai, who was in the Tokyo office of Joshiah Conder in 1887 when Conder was Japanese Government Architect. Sakurai subsequently came to England where he won the R.I.B.A.'s Donaldson Medal for 1889/1890 and was given the Architectural Association's Travelling Scholarship in 1891. This view dated 9 April 1891 comes from the *Builder* of 5 December 1891 (255x180).

The Deanery from Cloister Garth

The Old Deanery was originally the Abbot's quarters and then became the Prior's lodging and is connected with the west walk of the cloisters. The original building goes back to the Norman period, but now has its main frontage onto College Green and this is largely Victorian Gothic. It is now called Church House and is used for diocesan purposes. In 1940 the Dean's residence was moved to number one Miller's Green. This sketch of the Deanery from the cloisters by Herbert Railton comes from *Dreamland in History – the Story of the Norman Dukes* of 1891 by H. D. M. Spence (155x100).

This sketch by Herbert Railton shows the Cathedral tower as seen from the Old Deanery garden. It looks as if the Dean himself is talking to a diminutive member of his household. The drawing comes from *Dreamland in History – the Story of the Norman Dukes* of 1891 by H. D. M. Spence (170x115).

Another of Herbert Railton's drawings of the Old Deanery showing the whole facade. It also comes from *Dreamland in History – the Story of the Norman Dukes* of 1891 by H. D. M. Spence (85x110).

The Bishop's Palace was originally the Abbot's lodging before the Dissolution. It is an early fourteenth century complex rebuilt in 1862 by Ewan Christian and since 1955 has been the King's School. A new residence had been built for the Bishop in 1954 at the north-east corner of the Close and after 1986 this has become known as Bishopscourt. This view is an engraving of the building by James Sargant Storer after a drawing by his son Henry dated 1 January 1815 and comes from James Sargant Storer's *History and Antiquities of the Cathedral Churches of Great Britain* (117x85).

Two views of the Cathedral tower from the Palace Yard. In monastic days this building was part of the great hall on the north side of the Abbot's lodging and is now known as the Parliament Room. The view above is of 1896 by E. J. Burrow and comes from H. J. L. J Masse's *Cathedral Church of Gloucester* of 1898 (100x60). That below is of the early 1920s by A. Ward from his *Sketches of Gloucester* (115x100).

LLANTHONY PRIORY

A house of Austin Canons was founded by Hugh de Lacy at Llanthony in Gwent in the first decade of the twelfth century. Dugdale in the *Monasticon* describes it at that time as 'a dark valley crowned with airy woods and precipitous rocks almost inaccessible even to headlong beasts'. The house prospered until on the death of Henry I the Welsh started to raid the area and the Canons fled to the protection of the Bishop of Hereford. They were then offered land at Gloucester where a new foundation took place in 1136. All that now remains of the latter is a fragment of the gatehouse and part of the main arch surrounded by an industrial estate, a business park and the local football ground.

A view of Llanthony Priory in Gwent dated 14 May 1796. It comes from the *Antiquities of Great Britain* by Thomas Hearne and the engraver is William Bryne. The *Antiquities* was issued originally in parts and then in two volumes, the first from 1778 to 1786 and the second from 1796 to 1806 (190x255).

The ruins of Llanthony Priory in Gloucester when they formed part of a farm. Thomas Bonnor is the artist and engraver of this rural scene, which comes from Thomas Dudley Fosbroke's *Original History of the City of Gloucester* of 1819 (72x115).

Two views of the ruins of Llanthony Priory in Gloucester when part of a farm. Both views come from Francis Grose's *Antiquities* and the artist is Samuel Hooper. That above dated 15 December 1775 has John Roberts as the engraver (100x145) and that below dated 7 February 1776 is attributed to James Record (103x155).

Two further views of the ruins of Llanthony Priory in Gloucester. That above by Hugh Thomson is dated 1919, although not published until 1932 in *Highways and Byways in Gloucestershire* by Edward Hutton (110x95). That below is of the early 1920s by A. Ward from his *Sketches of Gloucester* (110x90).

- LLANTHONY ABBEY GATEWAY -

OTHER CHURCHES

Few medieval churches survive in Gloucester and they have all been considerably restored in the nineteenth century. St Mary de Crypt was largely rebuilt in the Perpendicular period and restored in 1844 by Dawkes and Hamilton. At St Mary de Lode a nave supported on cast iron columns was built into the original Norman work in 1826 by James Cook of Gloucester and there was a restoration in 1912. All that remains of St Michael in Southgate Street is the tower of 1485, as the rest of the church, which was rebuilt by Fulljames and Waller in 1851, was demolished in 1956. St Nicholas in Westgate Street is Perpendicular with a truncated spire lowered and repaired in 1783. There was a restoration in 1866 and again in 1927. St Margaret Wotton, formerly the chapel of the hospital of St Margaret and St Sepulchre, which passed to the United Almshouses was restored in 1875 by Waller and Son. St John the Baptist in Northgate Street is of 1732 to 1734 by Edward and Thomas Woodward of Chipping Campden, except for a fourteenth century west tower and spire and was restored in 1882.

The rest of the story is largely Victorian or later. All Saints in Lower Barton Street is by Sir George Gilbert Scott of 1875, Christchurch, Brunswick Square, by Rickman and Hutchinson of 1822, St James, Upton Street, of 1837 to 1841 by Sampson Kempthorne, St Mark, Kingsholme, of 1847 by Francis Niblett, St Paul, Stroud Road of 1882 to 1883 by C. N. Tripp, St Stephen, Linden Road, of 1895 by Walter Planck and the Mariners' Church by the Docks of 1849 by John Jacques.

The Roman Catholic Church of St Peter in London Road is of 1860 to 1868 by G. R. Blount and there are a number of non-conformist buildings, all of the nineteenth century except for the Unitarian Chapel of 1699 in Barton Street, which was altered in 1893 and demolished in 1968. The twentieth century is represented by S. Aldate, Finlay Road, of 1954 by Robert Potter and Richard Hare, St Barnabas, Tuffley, of 1939 to 1940, by N. F. Cachemaille-Day, St Catherine, Wotton, of 1915, by Walter B. Wood and St. Oswald, Coney hill, of 1939, by Ellery Anderton.

St Nicholas Church in Westgate Street. Thomas Bonnor is the artist responsible for this view and also the engraver and it is included in Thomas Dudley Fosbroke's *Original History of the City of Gloucester* of 1819. However, the drawing on which Bonnor made this view must have been sketched before 1783 when the spire was truncated and the top replaced with a coronet, pinnacles and the ball finial. In fact this view shows clearly how far the old spire was out of alignment. The building is sadly one of the many the Church of England has made redundant (120x170).

An etching by John Le Keux of a very attractive drawing of the now redundant church of St Nicholas, Westgate Street, dated 1 August 1828 by William Henry Bartlett with the figures added by W. H. Brooke. It shows a donkey with panniers, a flock of sheep, women selling produce from small tables and number of people in conversation in the background. The spire has its handsome coronet, pinnacles and ball finial put in place in 1783 when drastic repairs had to be carried out to the original structure. The view comes from John Britton's *Picturesque Antiquities of the English Cities* (215x135).

A drawing of St Nicholas Church, Westgate Street made by Sidney K. Greenslade during an Architectural Association sketching tour of 1895. It comes from the *Builder* of
24 August 1895 (185x105).

The Greyfriars Church has suffered a large number of changes over the centuries. About 1779 several residences were constructed within the shell of the building and in 1810 a substantial house was built into its west end. Also in the early nineteenth century another residence called Suffolk House was constructed close to the east end of the church. In the late 1960s Suffolk House was taken for the new market hall. The remains of the church were restored and the large house at the west end of the building was turned into a children's library. The view above with St Mary de Crypt Church in the background drawn and engraved by Thomas Bonnor comes from Thomas Dudley Fosbroke's *Original History of the City of Gloucester* of 1819 (102x155. The view below dated 24 August 1721 is a drawing by William Stukeley from his *Itinerarium Curiosum* of 1724, a rambling discourse on what he considered antiquarian curiosities. His accuracy was sometimes suspect and he attributes the building to the Whitefriars not Greyfriars. However the drawing does show the bowling green that was laid out in the early eighteenth century. The engraver of the view is E. Kirkhall (160x265).

St Mary de Crypt in Southgate Street is so called because it was built in the Norman period with an underlying crypt and had extensive restoration in 1844. This view was drawn and engraved by Thomas Bonnor and comes from Thomas Dudley Fosbroke's *Original History of the City of Gloucester* of 1819 (115x160).

This monument in St Mary de Crypt Church by Peter Scheemakers with a marble mourning female figure and portrait medallion is to Mrs Snell, who died in 1746. It too was drawn and engraved by Thomas Bonnor for Thomas Dudley Fosbroke's *Original History of the City of Gloucester* of 1819 (240x110).

St Mary de Lode Church is so called because of a near-by lode or passage over the Severn. It is a Norman church, which had a broad nave added in the early nineteenth century. It now stands in a modern precinct immediately west of the Abbey gate leading to the Cathedral. Above is a view drawn and engraved by Thomas Bonnor for Thomas Dudley Fosbroke's *Original History of the City of Gloucester* of 1819 (120x162). Below is a sketch by Hugh Thomson of the church in 1919, that was subsequently used in Edward Hutton's *Highways and Byways in Gloucestershire* of 1932 (100x90).

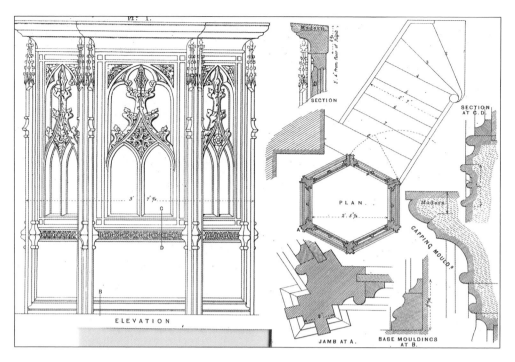

The pulpit in St Mary de Lode Church was restored with old wooden Gothic panels.
This measured drawing is by Francis Dollman and comes from his *Examples of Ancient
Pulpits Existing in England* of 1849 (Pulpit 135x100 Details 155x95).

This fourteenth century monument of a priest in eucharistic vestments under a muti-
lated arched recess is situated in the chancel of St Mary de Lode Church. It is said to
be of William de Chamberlayne, who died in 1304. The artist and engraver of this
view is Thomas Bonnor and it comes from Thomas Dudley Fosbroke's *Original
History of the City of Gloucester* of 1819 (125x150).

St Michael's Church, Southgate Street, was demolished in 1956 except for the handsome tower of 1465. These two views drawn and engraved by Thomas Bonnor also come from Thomas Dudley Fosbroke's *An Original History of the City of Gloucester* of 1819 showing the building in happier days when it was complete (south view above 120x170 north-west view below 120x165).

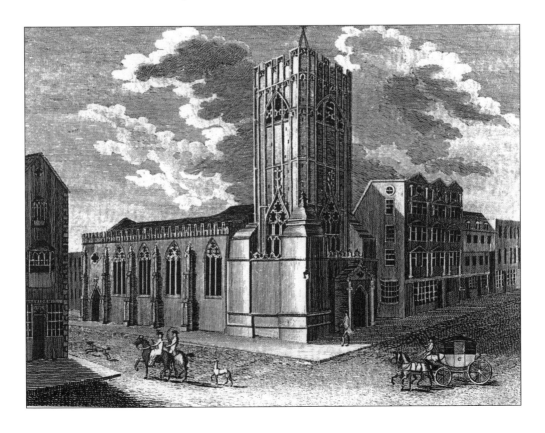

The 1465 tower of St Michael's Church drawn by G. G. Woodward in July 1883. It appears in volume 4 of the Architectural Association's *New Series of Sketch Books* (370x250).

Another view of the tower of St Michael's Church, as seen by Sidney K. Greenslade during an Architectural Association sketching tour in July 1895. It comes from the *Builder* of 24 August 1895 (190x135).

St John the Baptist Church, Northgate Street, was designed by Edward and Thomas Woodward of Chipping Campden and it was built between 1732 and 1734. Above is a view drawn and engraved by Thomas Bonnor for Thomas Dudley Fosbroke's *Original History of the City of Gloucester* of 1819 (125x170) and below a drawing from a similar viewpoint, but now surrounded by other buildings, by Sidney K. Greenslade in July 1895 during an Architectural Association sketching tour. The drawing comes from the *Builder* of 24 August 1895 (160x130).

A splendid baroque monument on the north wall of the sanctuary of St John the Baptist Church by Reeve of Gloucester. It is an above the waist effigy of Thomas Price, who died in 1678 and besides being Mayor of Gloucester was also Master of Horse to Charles I. He oozes the well-fed confidence of an obviously very important person. The representation is drawn and engraved by Thomas Bonnor for Thomas Dudley Fosbroke's *Original History of the City of Gloucester* of 1819 (180x85).

From 1878 until his death in 1905 Frederick Sanham Waller was the Cathedral's resident architect and played a prominent part in Victorian restorations of the building. This view by him entitled the *Ancient Towers and Spires of Gloucester* comes from the *Builder* of 9 January 1875 (270x170). In the letter coding A is St Nicholas church, B St Michael's Church, C St Mary de Crypt Church, D St John the Baptist Church, E St Mary de Lode Church, F The Deanery, G The Chapter House, H Chapter House library, K Gateway to St Mary's Square, L Ruins of church of St Catherine (see also page 7) and M remains of the Infirmary (270x170).

ACKNOWLEDGEMENTS

The advice and assistance of a number of people is always necessary in compiling a work of this kind and I would like to acknowledge with grateful thanks help from the following institutions and people; the Society of Antiquaries for permission to reproduce material and especially the Librarian Bernard Nurse and his staff for meeting my requirements for books, housed often in rather distant parts of the Society's premises; the courteous staff of the London Library; my wife Marion for her expert advice as an architectural historian; Steven Pugsley and his staff at Halsgrove Publishing for encouragement in compilation; and finally, but not least, a special thanks to all those artists and engravers whose skill over the centuries has produced such a wealth of material to illuminate the past of the City of Gloucester.

Parts of the Cathedral from Thomas Dudley Fosbroke's *Original History of the City of Gloucester* of 1819. No artist is given, but the engraver is Philip Audinet. Number one is the nave, number two the crypt, number three the whispering gallery below the eastern window forming a corridor between the north ad south triforium, number four is the north side of the west front, number five is the reliquary screen and number six is vaulting in the cloisters (whole engraved plate 180x100).

Parts of the Cathedral of Gloucester.

SUGGESTIONS FOR FURTHER READING

Alarge number of books and periodicals are mentioned in the body of the text and it seems pointless to repeat them here. Readers will make their own judgements about whether they wish to consult them further and in event they naturally vary widely in value, accuracy and usefulness.

For biographical information in general the *Dictionary of National Biography* and *Who Was Who* are essential. More specialist works I have found useful are Simon Houfe's *Dictionary of Nineteenth Century British Book Illustrators* (revised edition 1996) and Ronald Russell's *Guide to Topographical Prints* (1979), but above all Bernard Adams' *London Illustrated 1604-1851* (1983). This outstanding work of scholarship deals not only with exclusively London material, but also publications covering the whole country that have London sections, and therefore includes a mass of useful detail abut artists and engravers found in the present volume.

For early architects Michael Hicks' *Who's Who in Late Medieval England 1272-1485* (1991) and John Harvey's *English Medieval Architects – A Biographical Dictionary* (1984) are helpful. Sir Howard Colvin's *Dictionary of British Architects 1600-1840* (revised edition 1993) is indispensable and the *Dictionary of British Architects 1834-1900* (1993) brings the story up to the end of the nineteenth century. The *Gloucestershire – The Vale and Forest of Dean* volume in the *Buildings of England* series of 1970 by David Verey is still relevant, although now needs updating in the same way that has been done for the companion volume on the Cotswolds.

Volume four of the *Victoria Country History of Gloucestershire* is devoted exclusively to the City of Gloucester (1988) and has a mass of informative detail and so also has David Welander's the *History, Art and Architecture of Gloucester Cathedral* (1991).

The so called Pentrice bracket in the south transept of the Cathedral resembling a builder's square. Two curiously positioned figures support it, the lower with a bag at his waist said to be a master builder with his son or apprentice. Very much more prosaically it is probably just a bracket to take a light fitment. It is drawn and engraved by Orlando Jewitt for Richard John King's *Handbook to the Cathedrals of England* of 1865 (90x70).